CHRIS JERICHO

BEST IN THE WORLD

by Pete Delmar

Consultant:
Mike Johnson, Writer
PWInsider.com

CAPSTONE PRESS
a capstone imprint

Velocity is published by Capstone Press,
1710 Roe Crest Drive, North Mankato, Minnesota 56003.
www.capstonepub.com

Library of Congress Cataloging-in-Publication Data
Delmar, Pete.
Chris Jericho : best in the world / by Pete Delmar.
pages cm. — (Velocity. pro wrestling stars)
Includes bibliographical references and index.
Summary: "Describes the life and career of pro wrestler Chris Jericho"—Provided by
publisher.
ISBN 978-1-4296-9972-3 (library binding)
ISBN 978-1-4765-3582-1 (ebook pdf)
1. Jericho, Chris—Juvenile literature. 2. Wrestlers—Canada—Biography—Juvenile
literature. I. Title.
GV1196.J47D45 2014
796.812092—dc23 [B]   2013009487

Editorial Credits
Mandy Robbins, editor; Heidi Thomson, book designer; Sarah Bennett, set designer;
Laura Manthe, production specialist

Photo Credits
AP Images: Rick Scuteri, 23; Getty Images, 14, Ethan Miller, cover, Frank Micelotta, 12;
Globe Photos: Alpha, 9, John Barrett, 5, 21; iStockphotos: albertc111, 13; NBC via Getty
Images: NBCU Photo Bank/Paul Drinkwater, 41 (The Tonight Show); Newscom: SIPA/
McMullan Co, 38, Splash News/Octavio R Vera Jr, 39, ZUMA Press/Globe Photos/John
Barrett, 25, ZUMAPRESS.com/Matt Roberts, 27, ZUMAPRESS.com/ Toronto Star/Ron
Bull, 36-37, ZUMAPRESS.com/WWF/UPN-TV, 31, ZUMAPRESS.com/Z Sports Images,
18, 33; Photo by Wrealano@aol.com, 15 (top), 20, 30, 34, 45 (bottom); Shutterstock:
413x4sha, 17 (limo), Andy Lidstone, 6 (right), Anthony Berenyl, 17 (fireworks), bioraven, 8,
George Koroneos, 16, Keith Tarrier, 6 (left), Michael Pettigrew, 6-7 (hockey player), Molodec,
42, Robyn Mackenzie, 5, s_bukley, 45 (top), Sebastian Kaulitzki, 15 (x-ray), Sergiy Telesh,
24, Szantai Istvan, 10-11 (background), Tatiana Popova, 44 (book), txking, 43, Viachaslau
Kraskouski, 44-45 (background and frames), vipflash, 40-41 (background), Volina, 6-7 (map),
yanugkelid, 39; (red curtain); Wikimedia: Fatima, cover, 1 (background), GeeFour, 28, Simon,
19, Mshake3, 11

Artistic Effects
Shutterstock

Printed in the United States of America in North Mankato, Minnesota.
032013   007223CGF13

TABLE OF CONTENTS

INTRODUCTION:
COUNTDOWN TO Y2J

In 1999 everyone was talking about "Y2K." That was the popular term used to signify the upcoming year 2000. At the stroke of midnight between these two years, the 1900s were laid to rest. A new **millennium** began.

At about the same time, an exciting new wrestler blasted onto the World Wrestling Federation (WWF) scene. Before he even showed up, the buzz was on in the world of pro wrestling. WWF promos showed a "countdown to the new millennium." But the clock wasn't counting down to January 1, 2000. Rather, it was counting down to August 9, 1999. There was also talk about the Millennium Man. What did it all mean?

The man in question was Chris Jericho. He called himself Y2J. Chris was aiming to take the pro wrestling world by storm as the WWF's Millennium Man. The countdown clock on the commercials was marking the moment of his first appearance in the WWF ring.

That moment finally occurred on August 9, 1999. Since then Chris has been a pro wrestling powerhouse. His amazing wrestling skills, good looks, and bad-boy antics in the ring have brought him fame and fans. Y2J wasn't just a year-long phenomenon. Chris Jericho has turned out to be an enduring pro wrestling star.

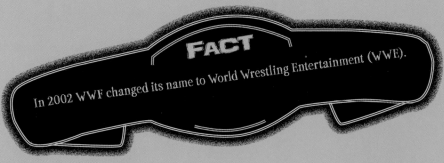

FACT

In 2002 WWF changed its name to World Wrestling Entertainment (WWE).

millennium—a period of 1,000 years

CHRIS JERICHO'S STATS

REAL NAME
Chris Irvine

HEIGHT
6 feet (183 centimeters)

WEIGHT
226 pounds (103 kilograms)

SIGNATURE MOVES
Codebreaker, Walls of Jericho

CHAPTER 1:
LIFE BEFORE JERICHO

Most of Chris Jericho's fans know he grew up in Canada. But what some might not know is that he was actually born in the United States. Chris is a legal citizen of both Canada and the United States. He was born Christopher Keith Irvine on November 9, 1970, in Manhasset, Long Island, New York. At the time his father, Ted Irvine, was a well-known pro hockey player with the New York Rangers.

Ted retired from hockey in 1977 and moved the family to Canada. They settled in Ted's hometown of Winnipeg, Manitoba.

Growing up Chris had a lot of interests and a lively imagination. He loved playing the game *Dungeons and Dragons* and had a collection of *Star Wars* and *Star Trek* action figures. Chris was also a huge fan of the rock bands The Beatles and Kiss. As he grew up, sports and rock music became a focus of Chris' life.

Kiss

The Beatles

MaDE In ManHaSSEt

Manhasset is a wealthy community on the north shore of Long Island. It's so small that it's not even officially a town, but a hamlet. For a place so small, Manhasset has been the home to an overwhelming number of stars. Celebrities who've called Manhasset "home" include baseball players José Reyes and Jason Marquis. Rapper and actor LL Cool J was also a Manhassett resident, as was NFL star and actor Jim Brown.

• WINNIPEG

• MANHASSET

FACT

Chris started watching pro wrestling on TV with his grandmother.

A PASSIONATE ATHLETE

Chris went to high school at Westwood Collegiate in Winnipeg. There he put a lot of energy into sports. Chris made all-star status on the hockey and water polo teams.

After graduating in 1988, he pursued a creative communications degree at Red River Community College. But what Chris really wanted was to be a pro wrestler. He'd caught the wrestling bug at the age of 7 by watching weekly matches on TV at his grandparents' house. But in college Chris worried that he wasn't big enough to wrestle professionally. That was until he saw Owen Hart in a match. Hart wasn't big and beefy either, but his acrobatic moves made him a star. It was eye-opening for Chris.

"It might as well have been a bolt of lightning sent straight from the heavens above. I didn't just want to be a wrestler ... I had to be a wrestler."
—Chris Jericho on the influence Owen Hart's wrestling had on him (A Lion's Tale: Around the World in Spandex)

After graduating college with honors in 1990, Chris headed straight for Okotoks, a small town outside Calgary, Alberta. That's where Owen's dad, Stu Hart, ran the Hart Brothers' Pro Wrestling Camp.

Owen Hart dominating his opponent, Papa Shango, at a match in London, England

TRAINING FOR THE FUTURE

The Hart family was famous in the world of pro wrestling. Owen and Bret Hart were the most famous of the eight Hart brothers. Chris had faith he'd get the kind of wrestling education he needed at the Harts' wrestling school. He was right.

Chris joined the Harts' program at the end of June 1990. He quickly befriended another member of that summer's training group, Lance Storm. They soon established themselves as the top two students and graduated in mid-September of 1990.

FIRST PRO MOMENT

After his training, Chris was eager to wrestle as a pro. And in only a few weeks he had a match scheduled. He made his professional **debut** on October 2, 1990. The gig was in the small Canadian town of Ponoka, Alberta. His opponent was none other than his new friend Lance Storm. About 100 people attended, and Chris got paid $30. It wasn't much, but it was a real wrestling match and real money. Following that first match, the two men wrestled frequently, both against each other and as a **tag team**.

debut—someone's first public appearance

tag team—when two wrestlers partner together against other teams

Lance Storm, 2007

CHAPTER 2:
LIFE ON THE WRESTLING CIRCUIT

After his debut Chris spent most of his time wrestling in random matches in both Canada and the United States. But he was ambitious. His ultimate dream was to make it into the top wrestling promotion company in the world—the WWF. He knew he'd have to work hard to get there. In the meantime, he was willing to wrestle wherever he could to build his reputation as a skilled pro wrestler.

Throughout the 1990s Chris worked on improving his wrestling skills. He wrestled with companies in the United States, Canada, Japan, and Mexico.

In Mexico Chris learned a high-flying acrobatic type of wrestling that suited his lightweight, athletic body. He soon became known for bounding to the ring's top rope and sailing through the air at opponents. This style gave his matches a gymnastic flair. Fans loved it!

EARLY WRESTLING VENUES

DatE	PROMOtion	LOCatiOn
Oct. 1991	Frontier Martial Arts Wrestling [FMW]	Japan
Nov.–Dec. 1992	Federación International de Lucha Libre (FILL)	Monterrey, Mexico
April 1993	Empresa Mexicana de Lucha Libre (EMLL)	Mexico City, Mexico
Feb. 1996	Extreme Championship Wrestling (ECW)	United States
Aug. 1996	World Championship Wrestling (WCW)	United States

A DREAM WITHIN REACH

Between 1990 and 1998, Chris moved steadily up the ranks of pro wrestling. After about six months with Extreme Championship Wrestling (ECW), he signed with World Championship Wrestling (WCW) in 1996. Chris' career was well-established by then. But after more than two years with that company, he felt like he had stalled. He wasn't getting the big opportunities he'd expected at WCW. It looked to him like his career was going nowhere.

Chris considered a new approach. He turned from **babyface** to **heel**. After every loss he would throw a giant temper tantrum. He'd shout insults at the crowd and be as obnoxious as possible. Fans went crazy for it.

FOOLISH DECISION

When Chris stepped into the ring on
August 5, 1994, he had a broken arm. He'd
gotten the injury during practice. But Chris felt
like he had to wrestle that night. He was scheduled
to wrestle in an event called *Night of the Legends*.
Fans were excited to see him in a tag team showdown.
Chris went ahead with the match. Fortunately, no further
damage was done to his arm, but he still had to have surgery.
Chris later admitted that going into the ring with a serious
injury was a very foolish move.

babyface—a wrestler who acts as a hero
in the ring

heel—a wrestler who acts as a villain in
the ring

REACHING THE WWF

As a heel at WCW, Chris' popularity soared. It also got the attention of the WWF leaders.

In early 1999 Chris got an interview with Vince McMahon, the owner of WWF. Chris was a nervous wreck as he rode in a limo up to McMahon's Connecticut mansion. For Chris, it seemed his lifelong dream was at last within reach.

Vince McMahon, WWE owner

When the WCW managers discovered Chris' plans to make a move, they offered him close to $1 million to stay put. But money wasn't his main objective. He eagerly accepted a salary of less than half that to be part of WWF. On June 30, 1999, Chris signed with the WWF. He was soon part of WWF's *Raw* broadcast team, working live on TV. He'd finally managed to achieve one of his biggest childhood dreams.

LIVING THE WWF LIFE

Chris' first WWF appearance occurred in Chicago on August 9, 1999, during *Monday Night Raw*. When the countdown clock hit zero, fireworks erupted. There was Y2J, confronting an audience gone wild—and living his dream.

Chris was impressed by the way the WWF wrestlers were treated. They had hairdressers and makeup people. They rode everywhere in limos. Unfortunately, Chris didn't get a great start in the company. Chris' whining, obnoxious heel character that had been so popular at WCW was a big flop at WWF. Both the WWF fans and Chris' fellow wrestlers were totally turned off by the whiny weakling in the ring. Chris got the message and quickly turned tough. He began playing a mean-talking menace in the ring. It was a good move. Fans and fellow wrestlers began to like Y2J. Before long he was in the WWF spotlight.

REAPPEARANCES

Chris has been a superstar during his WWE career. He's also dropped out of the spotlight more than once to pursue other interests. But he's always returned—so far.

GUESS WHO'S BACK

Chris disappeared from the WWE scene in August 2005 and didn't return until November 2007. During his over-the-top reappearance, he wore a silver vest and a trendy new haircut. In the ring he riled up the fans by shouting, "This is the second coming of Y2J!!"

BACK AGAIN

One of Chris' most memorable returns to wrestling took place on the night of January 2, 2012. This time he'd been gone for 15 months. Weeks before his return, WWE began running haunting promos promising a "mystery superstar" soon to come. On January 2, the stadium lights suddenly went out during a televised *Raw* event. A sparkle of silver glittered in the darkness. With a blast of fireworks, the lights finally shot back on. A bare-chested Chris Jericho with a glittering, lit-up jacket swaggered onstage. Chaos erupted among the thousands of fans in attendance.

After 15 months gone, Y2J's sudden appearance rocked the house. But then he pulled the most outrageous heel trick of all time. After whipping the crowd into a frenzy, he left without saying a word. He simply strutted offstage. Fans were outraged. Chris had left WWE as a babyface. But now he was back, a bigger heel than ever.

CHAPTER 3:
SIGNATURE STYLE

Over his long career as a pro wrestler, Chris Jericho has had a few major style shifts. His physical appearance has changed. He's been through more than a few name changes. He has frequently introduced new songs to use as his signature music. Here's a glimpse down memory lane—Y2J-style.

1990 PRO DEBUT LOOK

black and yellow tights

matching wristbands

• black leather boots

1992 TAG TEAM LOOK

• swirly-patterned black and white tights

• waist-long black jacket with very long rainbow-colored fringe

JULY 1992 PHOENIX LOOK

• mask with feathered headdress

• strap-on wings with colorful, sparkling stripes

LATE 1990S WCW HEEL LOOK

- hair in a topknot
- long sideburns
- elbow-length gloves
- white leather vest with a portrait of himself on the back

1999 WWF DEBUT LOOK

- silver shirt

  hair in a topknot

  billygoat beard

FACT

Chris first came on the wrestling scene with long, blond hair. By 2005 it was mid-length. On his return to the ring in 2007, Y2J's hair was short.

NAME CALLING

Chris came up with his in-ring name early on. Fresh out of wrestling school, he chose the name Jack Action. His wrestling pal Lance Storm hated it. Chris' next idea came from Luke Skywalker, the lead character in the movie *Star Wars*. Chris tried out Shawn Skywalker, Shane Skywalker, Seamus Skywalker, and even Shakira Skywalker. None hit the mark. Finally, Chris recalled a comic book character called Jericho. He remembered a song by the German metal band Helloween called "The Walls of Jericho." He thought "Chris Jericho" had a nice ring to it.

FACT

Occasionally, Chris has had trouble with people getting his ring name wrong. In one instance before he was famous, the *Calgary Sun* newspaper ran a wrestling event ad that printed Jericho's name as "Chris Cherrykoo."

Though he chose "Jericho" early on, Chris has gone by several other names and nicknames throughout his career.

NAME	WHERE
Corazón de León	Mexico
Lion Do	Japan
Super Liger	Japan
Lion Heart	WCW
Ayatollah of Rock N Rolla	WCW heel phase and WWE
Sexy Beast	WWE
King of the World	WWE

HELLO my name is

Chris gives Edge a knee to the face during their 2010 *WrestleMania* match.

While wrestling in Mexico, Chris used different Spanish names. Mexican people had difficulty pronouncing the word "Jericho." He was most familiar as Corazón de León, or Lion Heart.

23

A ROCKIN' HEEL

Although Chris has played a babyface over the years, his true genius has been in building his heel image. He came on the WWF scene promoting himself as the "savior" of Vince McMahon's operation. After returning to the wrestling ring in December 2007, he was being called the most hated heel in wrestling. His fans love to hate him—and Chris loves it!

ROCKING INTO THE RING

Chris has tried a lot of different styles when it comes to his entrance music and other signature tunes. His main theme music is "Break the Walls Down" by WWE composers Jim Johnston and Anthony Martini.

Here are a few other songs he's rocked to in the wrestling arena over the years.

- "Danger Danger" by Rock America

- "Electric Head Pt. 2 (The Ecstasy)" by White Zombie

- "Soul Crusher" by White Zombie

- "King Of My World" by Saliva

- "Crank The Walls Down" by Maylene and the Sons Of Disaster

FACT

Chris is a heavy metal fanatic. His personal playlist includes bands such as Metallica, Iron Maiden, Kiss, and Galactic Cowboys.

"Every time I go to the ring, I consider it a big party and I'm the party host."
-Chris Jericho in a 2000 interview with the *Winnipeg Sun*

CHAPTER 4:

BUSTIN' THE MOVES

Chris has been called "the Man of 1,004 Moves." He has strong technique and high-flying skills. Check out a few of Chris' most well-known moves.

LIONSAULT

Chris runs toward the ropes and jumps onto the middle rope. He grabs the top rope with both hands and does a backflip, twisting in midair. Chris flies through the air and lands on his opponent.

TIGER SUPLEX

When Chris' opponent has his back toward him, Chris hooks his arms around and under his opponent's arms. Then Chris flips over backward into a bridge, slamming his opponent's upper body into the mat.

DOUBLE UNDERHOOK BACKBREAKER

Chris faces his opponent. He forces the opponent's chin down so that the other man's chin is pressed against his own chest. Then Chris wraps his arms under his opponent's arms, forcing them up. In this position he lifts the other wrestler's body up, flipping him in midair before slamming him to the mat for a pin.

TRIPLE POWERBOMB

Facing his opponent, Chris forces the other wrestler's head between his legs. Then he wraps his arms around his opponent's waist and flips him upside down. Chris then swings his opponent's upper body up and slams it to the mat three times.

Chris prepares to slam CM Punk with a double underhook backbreaker.

FACT

The Lionsault is an extremely dangerous move. Chris warns people that they should not try it without a great deal of training.

FINISHING 'EM OFF

Every wrestler has a few wicked finishing moves too. These moves are meant to put an opponent down for good. Chris' favorite finishing move is the Walls of Jericho, but that's not his only finisher.

WALLS OF JERICHO

Chris turns his opponent facedown and grabs both of the other wrestler's legs. Chris then bends the legs back toward the opponent's face. He holds his foe down until he submits.

SPRINGBOARD CODEBREAKER

Chris balances on the ropes and then jumps sideways toward his standing opponent. He lands on his foe and pulls him down to the mat. As both men land, Chris stuns his opponent with a forceful double-footed kick.

ENZUIGIRI

Chris faces his opponent. He steps with his right foot and leaps into the air with his left foot forward. While in midair Chris swings his right leg forward and plants a painful kick on his opponent's head.

FACT

The Walls of Jericho is a variation on the wrestling move known as the Boston Crab. When Chris first began using it, he called it the Liontamer. Chris claims this move officially kicked his WCW career into high gear.

CHAPTER 5:
RIVALRY GONE WILD!

Bring on the drama! Chris has been **feuding** with many of the WWE's top wrestlers for years. Here are some highlights from his most intense rivalries.

1998 – DEAN MALENKO

In the late 1990s, Chris loved to brag about how much better he was in the ring than Dean Malenko. Malenko was called "the man of 1,000 holds." But Chris claimed that he was the master of 1,004 holds. The men feuded over who deserved the championship. Their battles delivered fans hours of entertainment. The crowning moment came when Chris was beaten by a masked opponent—who turned out to be Malenko.

DEAN MALENKO'S STATS

HEIGHT
5 ft, 10 in (178 cm)

WEIGHT
212 lbs (96 kg)

SIGNATURE MOVE
Texas Cloverleaf

2001 — THE ROCK

By 2001 Chris had turned babyface. At the time the Rock was another popular babyface. In fact the Rock was the fan-favorite, and Chris was an up-and-comer at WWE. But both were experts at verbally abusing their opponents. The Rock and Chris insulted each other back and forth for months. But Chris proved he had what it took to dominate the wrestling ring. He beat both the Rock and Stone Cold Steve Austin to claim the title of Undisputed WWE Champion.

THE ROCK'S STATS

HEIGHT
6 ft, 5 in (196 cm)

WEIGHT
260 lbs (118 kg)

SIGNATURE MOVES
Rock Bottom, People's Elbow

feud—to have a long-running quarrel with another person or a group of people

2002 – TRIPLE H

Chris' feud with Triple H went on for months. Triple H managed to end Chris' reign as Undisputed Champ, and Chris wasn't happy about it. The feud peaked at *Judgment Day 2002*. The two men fought a **Hell in a Cell** match, which Triple H ended up winning.

TRIPLE H'S STATS

HEIGHT
6 ft, 4 in (193 cm)

WEIGHT
255 lbs (116 kg)

SIGNATURE MOVE
The Pedigree

In a **Hell in a Cell** match, the entire ring and surrounding ringside are enclosed by a metal cage. This keeps wrestlers in and others out. These matches include weapons. Almost anything goes, even pipes, ladders, steel chairs, and more.

2008 – SHAWN MICHAELS

Chris and Shawn Michaels began feuding at *WrestleMania XIX*. Many fans consider this the best feud of Chris' career. During this feud Chris turned from a well-loved babyface into a cocky heel.

The feud began when Shawn Michaels faked a knee injury to win a match against Batista. Chris was the referee in the match. He stopped the match when Michaels appeared to be injured. But when he restarted the match, Michaels took Batista by surprise. He kicked him in the face with his supposedly injured leg.

Chris called Michaels out on his lie in an on-air interview. He became so angry, he smashed Michaels' head into a TV screen. The smash injured Michaels' eye. The two enemies met up again at the *Great American Bash*. During their match Chris went after Michaels' injured eye relentlessly. Chris was declared the winner.

A month later Michaels announced his retirement. Chris came out and took a swing at Michaels, but he ended up hitting Michaels' wife! Michaels decided not to retire and instead gave Chris a memorable pounding during their next match.

SHAWN MICHAELS' STATS

HEIGHT
6 ft, 1 in (185 cm)

WEIGHT
225 lbs (102 kg)

SIGNATURE MOVE
Sweet Chin Music

2012 – CM PUNK

In 2012 CM Punk was the reigning WWE Champion. He claimed he was the "best in the world." Chris decided to prove him wrong. He launched a verbal attack on Punk that led to several thrilling matches. The final match was at *WrestleMania*, where CM Punk came out the winner.

CM PUNK'S STATS

HEIGHT
6 ft, 2 in (188 cm)

WEIGHT
218 lbs (99 kg)

SIGNATURE MOVES
G.T.S. (Go to Sleep), Anaconda Vise

CHAPTER 6:
UNDISPUTED CHAMP

At the December 2001 WWF *Vengeance* event, Chris hit a historic high in his career. He was named wrestling's Undisputed World Heavyweight Champion. It was the first time that title had ever been given. Winning it meant Chris had claimed both the WCW Championship and the WWF Championship. He beat out Stone Cold Steve Austin, Kurt Angle, and the Rock to win the title. Today, after more than 20 years in pro wrestling, Chris is still one of the all-time greats. Check out how he made it to the top.

When he wrestled in Japan, Chris often faced off against Ultimo Dragón.

FIRST CHAMPIONSHIP WIN

Chris won his first championship belt in Mexico. It was the National Wrestling Association Middleweight Championship. He held it for nearly a year in 1993 and 1994 before Ultimo Dragón took it from him.

EARLY DEFENSE

One of Chris' greatest matches ever was in Ryogoku, Japan, against Ultimo Dragón in 1995. Chris defended his International Junior Heavyweight title in an exciting performance as 11,000 fans watched. Afterward he used the tape of that match anytime he needed to show off what he was capable of in the ring.

FAN APPEAL

Every year *Wrestling Observer Newsletter* (WON) and *Pro Wrestling Illustrated* (PWI) readers vote for their favorites in several categories. Since 1999 Chris has received top honors in many categories.

- 1999 & 2000: Most Underrated Wrestler (WON)
- 1999: Readers' Favorite Wrestler (WON)
- 2002 & 2008: Most Hated Wrestler (PWI)
- 2003, 2008, & 2009: Best on Interviews (WON)
- 2008: Match of the Year (WON)
- 2008: Feud of the Year (WON and PWI) with Shawn Michaels
- 2008 & 2009: Wrestler of the Year Lou Thesz/Ric Flair Award (WON)

FACT

Chris' fans call themselves "Jerichoholics."

BIG-TIME WINNER

The list of Chris' wrestling achievements is a long one. Since his entry into pro wrestling, the belts he has won have piled up quickly.

ECW TELEVISION CHAMPIONSHIP

WCW CRUISERWEIGHT CHAMPIONSHIP

WCW WORLD HEAVYWEIGHT CHAMPIONSHIP

WWE WORLD HEAVYWEIGHT CHAMPIONSHIP

EUROPEAN CHAMPIONSHIP

HARDCORE CHAMPIONSHIP

WWE TAG TEAM CHAMPIONSHIP

WWE UNDISPUTED CHAMPIONSHIP

InterContinental Champion Wins

Win #	Event	Date	Opponent
1st	*Armageddon*	12-12-99	Chyna
2nd	*Royal Rumble*	1-23-00	Chyna & Hardcore Holly
3rd	*Smackdown!*	5-4-00	Chris Benoit
4th	*Royal Rumble*	1-21-01	Chris Benoit
5th	*Raw*	9-16-02	Rob Van Dam
6th	*Raw*	10-27-03	Rob Van Dam
7th	*Unforgiven*	9-12-04	Christian
8th	*Raw*	3-10-08	Jeff Hardy
9th	*Extreme Rules*	6-7-09	Rey Mysterio

WWE INTERCONTINENTAL CHAMPIONSHIP

WORLD TAG TEAM CHAMPIONSHIP

FACT

Chris has won the Intercontinental Championship more times than any other wrestler.

CHAPTER 7:

BEYOND THE WRESTLING RING

As a kid Chris had three main goals for his life. He wanted to become a hockey star, a pro wrestler, and a rock star. He gave up his hockey dream when he realized he'd never be that great on skates. But Chris has made his wildest wrestling dreams come true. And he's even reached rock star status with his own band, Fozzy.

But that's not all of the ambitions Chris has achieved. Check out a few other avenues he's taken to make a name for himself.

AUTHOR

Chris has published two best-selling books about his wrestling career. They are *A Lion's Tale: Around the World in Spandex* (2007) and *Undisputed: How to Become a Champion in 1,372 Easy Steps* (2011).

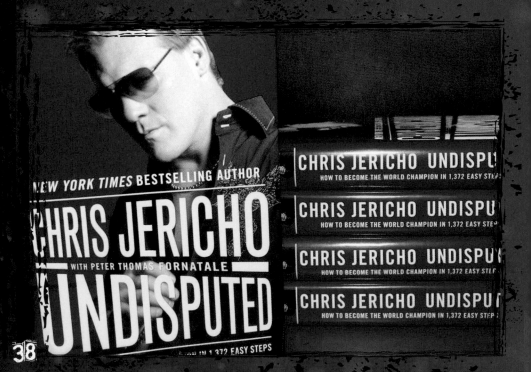

STAGE ACTOR

Chris starred as varnish salesman Jack Tisdale in the hit play *Opening Night* in Toronto, Ontario, Canada, in 2006.

RADIO DJ

In 2005 Chris hosted his own satellite radio show called "The Rock of Jericho."

A FAMOUS FACE

Chris' image has appeared on many products. His **avatar** first appeared in the 1998 video game *WCW Nitro*. Next he appeared in *WCW/nWo Revenge* and two other WCW games. His avatar also appeared in the game *WrestleMania 2000*. Chris has been the model for tons of action figures too. Many have been inspired by his biggest matches. Chris' image has even shown up on ice cream bars. His famous name has appeared on designer eyewear and bowling balls.

avatar—an electronic image that represents a person, often used in video games

TAKING ON HOLLYWOOD

Shooting promotional wrestling videos led to Chris' interest in acting. On one of his breaks from wrestling, he decided to try his luck in Hollywood. After taking some acting classes, he began to get parts. Check out some of his Hollywood roles:

 June 24, 2006: Chris played Tee-Dee in the SyFy Channel original movie *Android Apocalypse*.

 September 2009: Chris starred as Levi, a mean Ozark Mountains man, in the horror movie *Albino Farm*.

 May 2010: Chris had a **cameo** as a character named Frank Korver in the action-comedy *MacGruber*.

DANGER

 Aside from his wrestling career, Chris' biggest claim to TV fame is probably being part of *Dancing With the Stars*. He appeared on season 12, dancing with professional dancer Cheryl Burke.

COMEDY

In 2006 Chris got a chance to work with the famous L.A. comedy **improv** group the Groundlings. For about a year, he appeared fairly regularly in their Thursday night show, *Cookin' With Gas*.

cameo—a brief appearance by a celebrity

improv—a type of acting that is made up on the spot; short for "improvisation"

FACT

Chris has appeared on shows from numerous TV networks, including VH-1, MTV, and Fox. He's even worked as a TV game show host.

Chris had a visit with Jay Leno on the *Tonight Show* in 2011.

MUSIC VIDEO DIRECTOR

In 2000 Chris directed *Unleashed, Uncensored, Unknown*. The film was a comedic documentary featuring his band, Fozzy. Chris has also directed music videos that have aired on MTV and other music channels.

ROCK STAR

When Chris isn't wrestling, he's often living life as a rocker. It all began back in 1999, when he signed on with a band called Fozzy Osbourne, a tribute to rocker Ozzy Osbourne.

Fozzy Osbourne played 1980s-style hard rock and heavy metal music. Their songs included hits by Ozzy Osbourne, Iron Maiden, and Judas Priest. Chris never planned to make his gig with Fozzy Osbourne permanent. But he enjoyed it too much to quit. The next year Fozzy Osbourne shortened its name to just Fozzy. Chris became the band's **front man**, and he's been rocking with Fozzy ever since.

FOZZY LINEUP

lead singer	**Chris Jericho**
lead guitarist and backup vocals	**Rich Ward**
bassist	**Paul DiLeo**
drummer	**Frank Fontsere**
guitarist	**Billy Grey**

MAJOR FOZZY RELEASES

- **October 24, 2000**   *Fozzy*
- **July 30, 2002**   *Happenstance*
- **January 18, 2005**   *All That Remains*
- **January 26, 2010**   *Chasing the Grail*
- **August 14, 2012**   *Sin and Bones*

front man—the lead singer in a band who also interacts most with an audience

Chris rocks out for Fozzy fans at the 2012 Rockstar Uproar Festival in Nampa, Idaho.

FUTURE SO BRIGHT

These days Fozzy seems to be at the forefront of Chris' career. Wrestling has taken a back seat—at least for now. But he's focused on a couple other things as well.

> "I've done everything I could possibly do in wrestling. It's been great, but now Fozzy is kind of growing to be at the level where I am in wrestling, and Fozzy is what I wanna do."—Chris Jericho, in a 2012 interview with Fighting Spirit Magazine

SPORTS TRAINING CLUB OWNER

In January 2012 Chris became a co-owner of the D1 Sports Training and Therapy facility in Tampa, Florida. His partners are pro football player Tim Tebow, former pro football player Derrick Brooks, and pro baseball player Chipper Jones.

BOOK NUMBER THREE

Chris plans to have a new book come out in February 2014. He will probably be spending time promoting it.

FAMILY MAN

Chris married Jessica Lee Lockhart on July 30, 2000. His three kids are an important priority. They keep him close to home as much of the time as he can manage. Chris' son, Ash Edward Irvine, was born September 24, 2003. His twin daughters, Sierra Loretta Irvine and Cheyenne Lee Irvine, were born July 18, 2006.

What does the future hold for Chris Jericho? Will he remain Y2J, one of WWE's hottest stars? In the past his departure from the wrestling ring has never been permanent. Only Chris knows where wrestling fits into his future plans. But there's little doubt he has a promising future, no matter where he puts his attention!

GLOSSARY

avatar (AV-uh-tar)—an electronic image that represents a person, often used in video games

babyface (BAY-bee-fayss)—a wrestler who acts as a hero in the ring

cameo (KA-me-oh)—a brief appearance by a celebrity

debut (DAY-byoo)—a person's first public appearance

feud (FYOOD)—to have a long-running quarrel with another person or a group of people

frontman (FRUNT-man)—the lead singer in a band

heel (HEEL)—a wrestler who acts as a villain in the ring

improv (IM-prahv)—a type of acting that is made up on the spot

millenium (muh-LEN-ee-uhm)—a period of 1,000 years

signature move (SIG-nuh-chur MOOV)—the move a wrestler is best known for; sometimes called a finishing move

tag team (TAG TEEM)—two wrestlers who partner together against other teams

READ MORE

Brickweg, Jason. *Chris Jericho.* Pro Wrestling Champions. Minneapolis: Bellwether Media Inc., 2013.

Kaelberer, Angie Peterson. *The Fabulous, Freaky, Unusual History of Pro Wrestling.* Unusual Histories. Mankato, Minn.: Capstone Press, 2011.

Price, Sean Stewart. *Chris Jericho.* Stars of Pro Wrestling. Mankato, Minn.: Capstone Press, 2010.

INTERNET SITES

FactHound offers a safe, fun way to find Internet sites related to this book. All of the sites on FactHound have been researched by our staff.

Here's all you do:

Visit *www.facthound.com*

Enter this code: 9781429699723

INDEX